MY VERY OWN BOOK OF

ANCIENT EGYPT

Andrea M. Brida

Designed by

‌
- -

Life by the Nile

The ancient civilization of the pharaohs flourished by the banks of the Nile River in Egypt for more than 3,000 years. Flowing through inhospitable desert, the Nile flooded every year, depositing a thick layer of dark fertile silt over the fields. Without the annual flood, life would have been impossible.

Fish out of water
Children wore fish-shaped amulets in their hair, possibly to guard them against an accident in the Nile.

Lucky ring
This ring has a swiveling stone in the shape of a scarab. The underside of the scarab is carved with a good-luck design.

A royal vulture
The vulture on this mummy mask represented royalty. The Egyptian vulture still lives on the banks of the Nile River today.

Catch!
These colorful clay balls were sometimes filled with beads or seeds, so that they rattled when they were thrown.

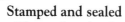

The river beat
Egyptians loved music. This is a model of a girl playing a harp. In real life she would rest the harp on a stand while she plucked the strings.

Stamped and sealed
The underside of scarab stamps would often include useful information that the owner could stamp on clay or papyrus.

All made up
Egyptians were lovers of beauty and fashion. Eye paint was worn by both men and women.

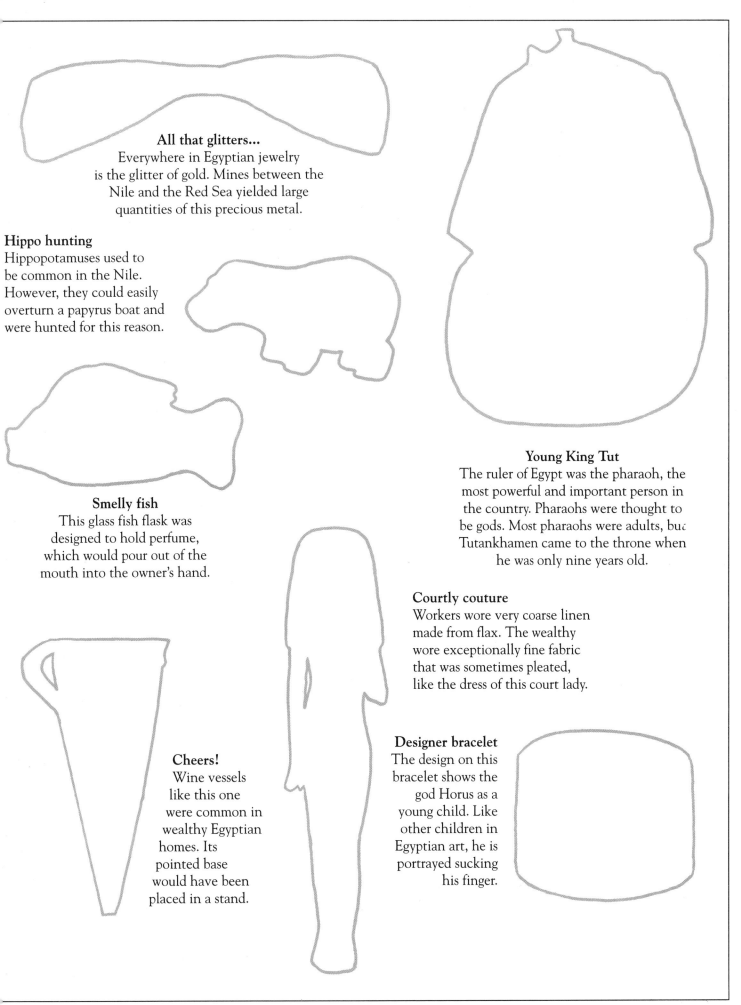

All that glitters...
Everywhere in Egyptian jewelry is the glitter of gold. Mines between the Nile and the Red Sea yielded large quantities of this precious metal.

Hippo hunting
Hippopotamuses used to be common in the Nile. However, they could easily overturn a papyrus boat and were hunted for this reason.

Smelly fish
This glass fish flask was designed to hold perfume, which would pour out of the mouth into the owner's hand.

Young King Tut
The ruler of Egypt was the pharaoh, the most powerful and important person in the country. Pharaohs were thought to be gods. Most pharaohs were adults, but Tutankhamen came to the throne when he was only nine years old.

Courtly couture
Workers wore very coarse linen made from flax. The wealthy wore exceptionally fine fabric that was sometimes pleated, like the dress of this court lady.

Cheers!
Wine vessels like this one were common in wealthy Egyptian homes. Its pointed base would have been placed in a stand.

Designer bracelet
The design on this bracelet shows the god Horus as a young child. Like other children in Egyptian art, he is portrayed sucking his finger.

Egyptian religion

Egyptians worshiped hundreds of different gods and goddesses, many of which were represented by animals. The sun god was the dominant deity, and he could take several different forms. The pharaoh Akhenaton banished all other gods during his reign, but his son Tutankhamen restored them when he came to power.

A very special scarab
This special scarab, placed over a pharaoh's heart, is inscribed with a spell to help the pharaoh through final judgment.

Everlasting power
The ankh was not only a symbol of everlasting life. It also indicated that the pharaoh who wore it had the power to give or take a life.

The healing eye
According to legend, Horus had his eye miraculously restored after a fight against evil. The eye of Horus, or wedjat eye, is connected with healing and protection.

The green god
The god Osiris was the god of vegetation and rebirth, especially in regard to the yearly flooding of the Nile. Green faces on mummy cases link the dead with this aspect of Osiris.

Holy beetle
The scarab, or dung beetle, symbolized the sun god Khepri.

Cat power
Bastet, daughter of the sun god, represented the power of the sun to ripen crops.

Big bird
Because the beak of the ibis was like a crescent moon, it became a symbol of the moon god Thoth.

Dog god
Animals were thought to be representatives or spiritual messengers of the gods. The jackal was sacred to Anubis, god of embalming.

Magic
Gods and magical symbols decorate this mummy case.

GODS

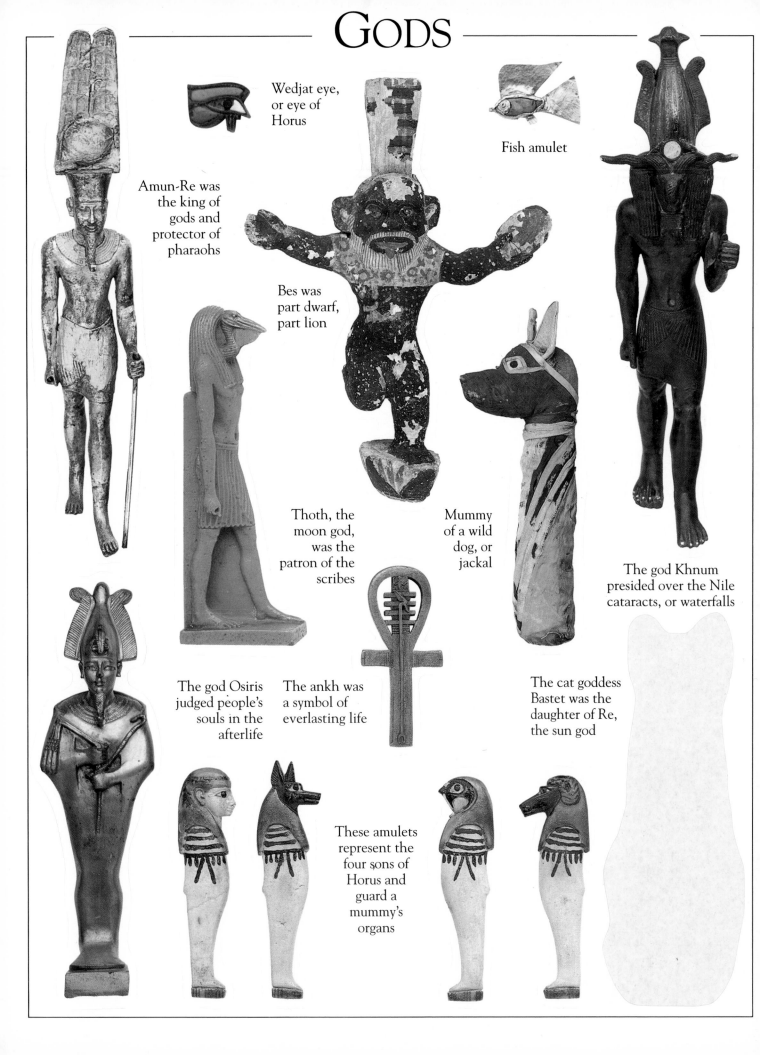

Wedjat eye, or eye of Horus

Fish amulet

Amun-Re was the king of gods and protector of pharaohs

Bes was part dwarf, part lion

Thoth, the moon god, was the patron of the scribes

Mummy of a wild dog, or jackal

The god Khnum presided over the Nile cataracts, or waterfalls

The god Osiris judged people's souls in the afterlife

The ankh was a symbol of everlasting life

The cat goddess Bastet was the daughter of Re, the sun god

These amulets represent the four sons of Horus and guard a mummy's organs

MUMMIES

This is an
unusual
mummy of
a dancer

Linen
holds
the mask
and chest
plate in
place

The pink
face shows
this is a
woman's
coffin

This wooden mummy
case is covered in gold

Inside this
wrapping
is a Roman
man who
had arthritis

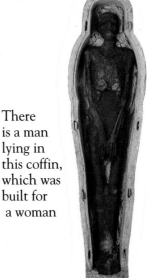

There
is a man
lying in
this coffin,
which was
built for
a woman

Cats,
sacred to
Bastet,
were
mummified
when they
died

This nest of mummy
cases belonged to a priestess

No one knows
the identity of
this mummy

The base of
the mummy
case is covered
with magic spells

Duamutef, a jackal, guarded the stomach

A ritual knife, with gold handle and flint blade

A mummy's organs were embalmed separately in canopic jars. This one represents the god Imsety, who guarded the liver

Qebehsenuef, a falcon, guarded the intestines

Hapy, a baboon, guarded the lungs

The wedjat eye, or eye of Horus

Head of a mummy

Shabti, or servant in the afterlife

These amulets protected the mummy

A mummy on its journey to the Duat

This bronze case held a mummified shrew mouse

This special scarab was placed over the heart of the pharaoh

Canopic jar, containing a large mummified liver

MUMMY MASKS

This elegant gilded mask was very popular in Egypt around 1,000 years ago

The mask's green face represents the god Osiris

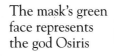

This carving shows a beautiful Egyptian face

Tutankhamen's mummy mask was made of solid gold

This wooden face was pegged onto a mummy case

When the Romans occupied Egypt around 2,000 years ago, portraits of the dead were painted on wood panels

This mask comes from the time of Tutankhamen, around 3,200 years ago

Glass eyes were added to this mask to create a more lifelike appearance

The vulture headdress on this mask suggests that the wearer may have been a princess

COLORFUL CASES

This case is
made from
cartonnage,
a kind of
papier-mâché

This amulet guarded the
mummy's intelligence

Magic
symbols
decorate
this case

Painted boards
were often put
on top of the
mummy

Rishi, or
feathered
mummy case

Mummy case of
Tjentmutengebtiu

Shabti
mummies

Mummy case from
Roman period

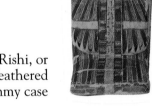

DAILY LIFE

Bracelet with lapis
lazuli scarab set in gold

Rings often
incorporated a
swiveling stone

These
balls are
made of clay

The ripples
in this fish flask
represent scales

Ground
minerals were
mixed with
water to make
eye paint and
then kept in
tubes like this

This wine
jar is made of
faience, obtained
by heating up
powdered quartz

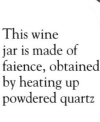

This royal bracelet shows the
god Horus as a young boy

This court
musician
has a wedjat
eye tattoo

Adorned with
flowers, this court
lady is wearing a
fine pleated
dress bordered
with a fringe

This lotus-shaped
makeup box has
a sliding lid

The scarab
beetle symbolizes
the sun god

The hippopotamus was an evil omen
because of its association with the god Seth

Underside of
scarab

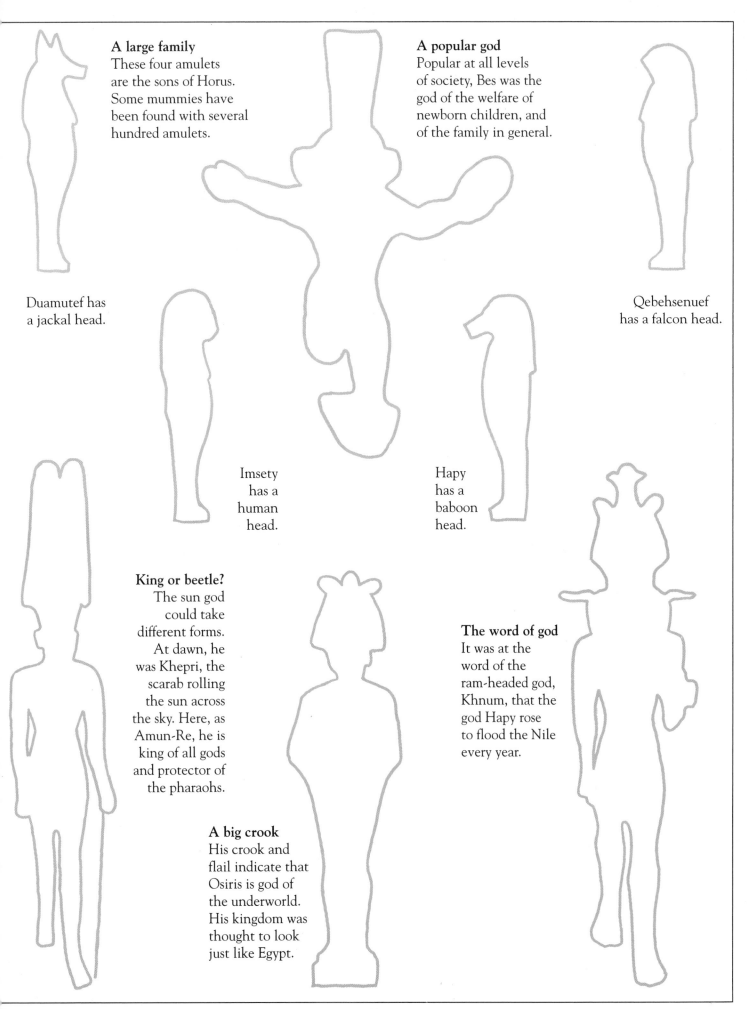

A large family
These four amulets are the sons of Horus. Some mummies have been found with several hundred amulets.

A popular god
Popular at all levels of society, Bes was the god of the welfare of newborn children, and of the family in general.

Duamutef has a jackal head.

Qebehsenuef has a falcon head.

Imsety has a human head.

Hapy has a baboon head.

King or beetle?
The sun god could take different forms. At dawn, he was Khepri, the scarab rolling the sun across the sky. Here, as Amun-Re, he is king of all gods and protector of the pharaohs.

The word of god
It was at the word of the ram-headed god, Khnum, that the god Hapy rose to flood the Nile every year.

A big crook
His crook and flail indicate that Osiris is god of the underworld. His kingdom was thought to look just like Egypt.

Death and burial

The process of mummification was intended to make an everlasting body out of a decaying corpse in order to provide the Ka, or spirit, with a home in the afterlife. The process lasted 70 days, after which the mummy was encased in coffins to ensure its safe journey to the afterlife. Mummies were entombed with animals, food, games, servants – anything that would make their future life more comfortable.

Typical features
This elegant gilded mask is rich in raised decoration, a feature typical of the Greek and Roman periods.

Unraveled
X-ray analysis meant that mummies could be electronically "unwrapped."

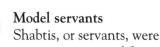

Model servants
Shabtis, or servants, were sometimes put in elaborate cases made to look like real mummy cases. This one is made of blue faience.

Three coffins full
This priestess had three coffins. This one, of gilded wood, is the most impressive.

Under wraps
Hundreds of yards of linen go into the wrapping of a mummy. As many as 20 layers of bandages and shrouds have been counted on one mummy.

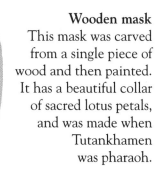

Wooden mask
This mask was carved from a single piece of wood and then painted. It has a beautiful collar of sacred lotus petals, and was made when Tutankhamen was pharaoh.

The tattooed dancer
Tattoos and markings on the wrappings of this mummy indicate that he was probably a dancer at religious ceremonies and banquets.

Tied up
After embalming and wrapping, a mask was fitted over the mummy's head. A chest plate and foot case were often added as well. These were held in place with bandages.

Up to the eyeballs
Eyes were destroyed by the preserving salts, so pads of linen were put in the sockets.

Duamutef

Imsety

Canopic containers
Any part of your body could be used in a spell against you, so everything needed special protection. Internal organs, which decayed quickly, were embalmed separately in canopic jars.

Cat mummy
Cats, sacred to the goddess Bastet, were mummified when they died.

Hapy

Qebehsenuef

The golden stab
The embalming incision was always made on the left side of the body. When the internal organs had been removed, the incision was covered with a plate decorated with a wedjat eye.

The unknown mummy
Ancient Egyptians went to great lengths to preserve their dead, but so many people were mummified that we do not know the names or identities of most of the mummies that survive today.

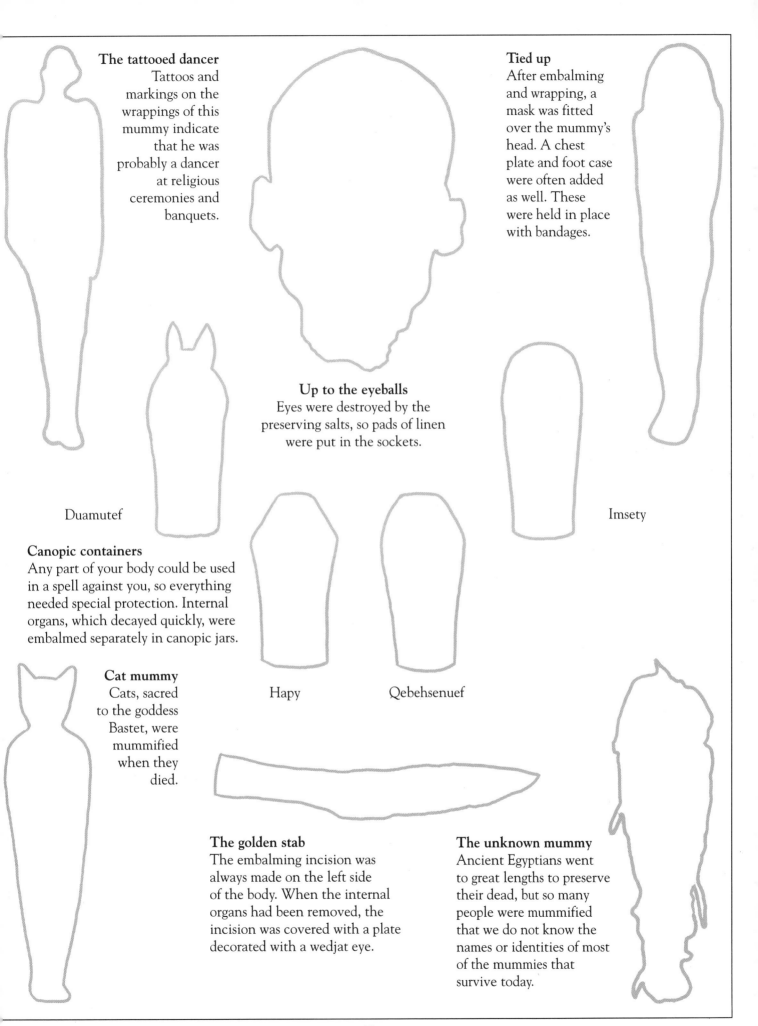

The afterlife

Below the Earth was Duat, the underworld. The way there was full of perils, but the right spells from the Book of the Dead could help you on your journey. In the Hall of the Two Truths, your heart was weighed to see if you had led a good life. If you had, you achieved everlasting life.

Mother's little helper
Models of servants were placed in the tomb to look after the mummy in the afterlife.

Board mummy
This mummy is carved from wood, plastered, and painted in relief.

Imitation boat
Funerary boats had a special design imitating the boat used by the sun god for his journey to the underworld.

Carton case
The mummy was placed inside the cartonnage case while the case was still damp and flexible. Once the case dried, it was laced up the back, sealing the mummy in.

A cozy nest
A mummy was laid in coffins or mummy cases to protect the body on its journey.

Forever beautiful
This blue faience makeup box is shaped like a stylized lotus plant.

Nail it down
The pegs on the sides of this base acted as nails, holding the lid snugly in place.